# Like As If

Poems by Bruce McRae

# Contents

## *"Existence Is Elsewhere"*

## *Light's Wedding*

## Conscience, with Fur

Comparisons are odorous.
> — Shakespeare

Metaphors have a way of holding the most truth in the least space.
> — Orson Scott Card

Poetry has become the higher algebra of metaphor.
> — Jose Ortega Y Gasset

Science is all metaphor.
> — Timothy Leary

Metaphors are dangerous.
> — Milan Kundera

Metaphors are much more tenacious than facts.
> — Paul De Man

A simile is said to be a short episode.
> — Samuel Johnson

In argument similes are like songs in love, they describe much but prove nothing.
> — Franz Kafka

Similes prove nothing, but greatly enliven and relieve the tedium of argument.
> — Robert South

Hyperbole, verging on histrionics. Hectoring lists. Mangled metaphors. Super-similes, which lean toward hysteria: as if 'like' and like 'as if'. A flying fortress of images and imagery. Wordplay. Cinematic mélange. A stand-up comic's throwaway one-liners. (Yes, humour, of the rubber crutch variety.) This collection's main theme concerns the pushing of poetic language to its extremes and is dedicated to all those who don't read poetry.

— Patrul Rinpoche

As in a magic show, things appear but have no reality of their own.

— Bruce McRae

I've never metaphor I didn't like.

— Bruce McRae

*for my little sister*

*"Existence Is Elsewhere"*

# Grass In My Hair

I was arguing
with the scarecrow.
His voice
was like a wall
of sand coming
closer and closer.
He had corn
on his breath
but no mouth
to speak of.
His mind
was a straw stalk
in the wind,
all the colours
of a golden
rainbow, there,
but not there,
even his pinstripes
soil-scented.
And I was saying
to the scarecrow,
"We end,
we begin."
I was telling him
the true names
of all the dead.
I was asking
a stupid question:
"Where's the crow
inside my head?"

Which he thought
quite funny,
a perpetual grin
on his dried lips,
his eyes seeing
into the far distance,
a tear forming
in the new silence
that summer, and he
impeccably dressed.

# Evictee

You mean the house inside the house.
You mean the mythmaker's lodgings,
with its many doors and million windows.

Which is the sea under the mountains
or a thirteen billion year old light ray.
Which is everywhere, like ancient snow.

Oh, but why didn't you say so?
You mean the house next door to the nothingness,
across the road from the flaming hospital,
by the perpetually exploding dancehall.

Where the carbon blobs happily dwell
and midnight barks like a dog.
Where the spectral sailors are knocking.

The house made of bones being broken.
The house of minds snapping.
The house where the World used to live,
until Tragedy stopped by for a while,
until Time spat out its toothpick.

I remember the blinds in the kitchen
coming down hard.
Like a fist on a table
or satellite crashing.
I remember there were dirt walls in the cellar
and an angry lightbulb on all night.
With vast continents

hidden under its floorboards,
Mr. and Mrs. Chemical, long dead now,
rearranging the grassblades,
old toys still in the yard,
bejeweled in the glistening rain,
the roadway passing
filled with the children's lost voices:
like a skip-rope-rhyme
in my feverish mind.

# Auspicious

The weather promises to change
from man to animal.
Today's forecast is absence,
with a chance of longing.
In the east, flying horses
and a scattering of flowers.
From the west, incursions,
barbarous hordes, black ice.

The weather changes its mind,
abandons its principles,
is forced to choose between
darkness and light.
They're predicting tons
of tons and long cold showers.
They say it might break,
but we're in for a hard spell.

Today's weather is being
brought to you by sponsors
who'd rather you didn't
put their names around.
Listener, the sea is rising
up out of its empty shell.
For all its talk of courage,
the wind is turning.

# The County Fair

My father traveled to the far solitudes.
My father ate religion.
My father was a monkey riding show ponies.

He'd come home years later.
He had a jezebel at every gas station.
He had a fist like a bus.

Often mother would leave out cookies and cream.
She'd bundle us under her apron.
She exhausted her plenitudes and riches.

O daddy-o, like an imaginary friend.
Like a candle puffed out at both ends.
Like Cro-Magnon man counting up to ten.

So then mum buried herself.
She took to the high wires and two fridges.
She petted the boarder.

Not much fun for we thirteen kids.
Not much cop with these ciphers and struggling.
A hell of an example for the wee bairns.

I remember the Xmas tree on fire
and something being thrown from a bridge.
I remember the act of forgetting.

That there were questions we could never put to him.
The Cadillac shimmer.

His long black coat and his wicked glare.

And poor ma, with her head out the window.
Poor ma, embroiled with the children,
and her spirit broken.

# Bookworm

*"No furniture so charming as books."*
                    *—Sydney Smith*


A pen clogged with outer space.
Two sentences mud-wrestling.
King Myna, the grammarian,
sharpening a Phoenix's quill,
dipping into the ink of an apocalypse,
employing a catastrophic syntax,
a language with no word for *word*,
any sense of tense sent packing.

A mob of letters rioting,
looting vowels, ransacking verbs,
the downtown core burning
like a page in a novel.
Uptown yet to be written.

A cosmological penciling-in.
The scribblers' craft brought low,
writing like speech's silhouette,
then an adjective getting a last shot in,
a noun dragging a thumbnail
across its dirty great neck.

The bookworm turning.

# Blueprint

You talk about the soul
as if it were a gift
plucked from a snowbank.

You speak of the soul
as of it were the capstone
of an ivory pyramid.

As if the soul were an eye
on the wing, fire and feathers
smoking across the evening.

The soul, with its side kicked in,
batting its eyelashes violently,
up to its waist in spiral water.

The soul, which has no soul.
The soul shoved down a neck.
The soul, its voice like a nail-file.

In the book I read you said
the soul is a cage of claws and jaws.
That the body is its bedroom.

You drew a rough-hewn circle,
explaining the soul's house
has no windows or doors.

God, you mentioned; *god god god*.
Architect of the soul.

Its almighty proofreader.

The one who put this mark on the wall
of my heart, who named the soul,
who declared its purpose.

Soul, like a bull's-eye on my chest.
Soul, its ton of talcum powder.
Its ghost haunting the mind's mansion.

And mine, which is dingy and bent.
And yours, its subtle theory.
And the beasts that you claimed had none.

So what hangs in the museum of time
is an instinctual death;
at the last gasp, the soul's blessing.

# This Word Has No Word For It

This word is unpronounceable.
Translated roughly,
it means a bluster of breath.
Spell it as you wish.

This is the first word in words.
It means love
in any language.
And rhymes with nothing.

This is a dirty word.
Nobody knows what it means.
Class, linguistics
is not an exact science.

The word for blood
actually tastes like blood,
a real jaw-breaker
better left unsaid.

And this word will get you killed.
You spit it at your enemies.
Repeat after me:
This is the word for silence.

# Little Wind

We begin with the still-beating heart of a dove,
which sounds much like rapturous applause.

We come to a pane of glass pitted by moonbeams;
as if starlight muted through a pitcher of cream.

In the meantime something like wind blowing out
of a desert canyon is blowing from out of a desert canyon.

If you'll turn to your left you'll find the world turning to the right.
You're approaching the centre; we are always coming to the centre
Always we are coming to a precipitous edge –
a slippery acre, tacky with both ecstasy and dread.

Next, a chapter some will find indigestible.
You've been under the constant influence of its shining mountain
one emotion wearing the coat of another emotion,
a little wind whispering *spiritus spiritus* . . .
Let's call this a well, shall we, or a quilt of crimsony gravitas.
It puts me in mind of arms crossed over the chest of Pharaoh.
Which is like sunlight eating away at a stone.
Which is what lives under the pebbles on the planet Mercury.

Behind us, a ravenous mouth of one some would call Death.
Below, a wheel composed of pollen and shame.
Over our heads, the air temperature falling.
But it's what lies ahead that must most concern us;
an amorphous thundercloud composed of colour and light.

This may be a thought reflecting on a mirror.

This could possibly be a memory forgetting itself.
Or it might be nothing more than a dream turning over in bed,
its heart still beating, its eyes mad-red,
its message incomprehensible.

# On A Chair

I'm sitting on a chair made out of tindersticks and time.
I'm sitting alongside a curtainwall of pale water and light.
Sunset is pouring out its glass of red wine.
The stars are hornets rustling their bedclothes
or the sister Fates making sparks by rubbing their thighs.
The moon is a motherly button.

I'm sitting inside a circle of crushed beetles' wings,
translating salt into a palatable sugar,
spinning yarn out of my abdomen,
retracing the patient constellations.

I'm sitting. And I'm thinking.
I'm thinking about sitting and thinking.
About fingers, jawbones, instances.
Where I'll sleep tonight, I've yet to decide,
I'm so taken up with just *sitting*.
On a throne shaped like a milking stool.
On a beach chair folded into seven dimensions.
There's a moist-warmed mist around my ankles.
My pulse is tangled in fibrous wire and snares.

In truth, I've been sitting here for several millennia,
my stones whistling in the relentless heat.
The Blue Nile and White Nile are meeting
here, just under my black feet.
There's interference on nineteen frequencies.
The vibrations are post-apocalyptic.
I sense them with my million moth-antennae.
It's a message repeating itself in the far future.

My molars are rattling in sympathy.
My bloodstream jingle-jangles unobtrusively.

Just sitting and sitting . . .
Listening to the underscore of earthly music.
Twisting the brindled locks in my hair.
Gazing out the window at a mind full of sky,
the years nibbling on the wheels of my chair,
the years forever unsatiated, the smoke in their mouths
a new language taking shape, truth divided by lies,
lost love divvying out its smaller portions,
life's door closing like an eye, like Horus's eye,
that was lost in battle, his sacrifice symbolic,
the pillar of Osiris rising . . .

## One Night In Ten

It was the eleventh day of Christmas.
I awoke to the sound of pins marching.
The dark was raining its felt hats.

I rose several times, uninventing the bed.
All through the house I felt it,
the presence of another, of another's hands
making little tea cakes from dreamy remnants.

I walked amongst a surplus of darkness,
room to room, floating several inches in the air.
Mice were stirring their cauldron of heads.
I sensed the unliving conferring with roaches.
The neighbours' dreams were playing loudly next door.
Peeking past a curtain, I saw the stars scratching.
I thought of frozen cubicles, cubes of blue ice,
a thousand innermost thinkings.

The moon had been replaced by an errant cloud,
by a streetlight on the fritz down the road.
In the wooden houses I could hear ears listening
to the long scraping of year unto year.
A summer's day flashed its breasts in my mind.
Perhaps I was dreaming, like a fish, with my eyes open;
that I was sleeping like a horse, standing up.

This revelry was broken by a crack in the pillow.
A voice called to me. Like a flower opening.
Like a door pushed shut by the passing wind.

I drifted days, or seconds, on the sea of my breaths.
I returned to the scene of my accidental birthing.
The bed whirled in tempests of quietude.
Many times I lay down before closing my eyes,
my mind's eyes, which went everywhere
and saw nothing.

# The Clouds Bursting

The night in smudged charcoal.
Thunder devouring what remains unseen.
Lightning cutting its own throat.

I remember a thick slobber of rain.
It was coming down hard, relentlessly,
like celestial spit or cherubs pissing.

Brother, I was building a boat out of love.
For nails, I was pinching the wind.
For my sails, torn thunderheads.
My rudder the sea-surge gushing ashore.

I remember a pillar of darkness,
concern carving its idolatrous god,
worry wringing its handbell.
Sister, how well I recall
thunderbolts sharpening themselves
on the whetstone of my thinking.
The ocean tearing sheets.
Our town barging miles inland.
The houses rocking.

It was like waking up in one dream
and falling asleep in another.
It was like swimming into the underworld
or a held breath in the womb.
Everything moving, everything alive . . .

But I need you to understand the rain

was a symbol and not a sign.
That I had one foot in the afterlife
and the other in prehistory.
That there was no night, no rain, no I.
That a storm never ends
in a world neverending.

# A Little Chat With Ourself

I'm talking to you through a rip in the seaside,
out of a warmed dent in the passing nothingness,
from behind a loop of tightly woven angel-hair.

I'm talking to you, and the wind is rubbing a cornfield.
I'm telling you the sun is sawing with its right hand.
That the moon is a knothole in God's coffin,
the stars His marred and excitable match-heads.

I'm going along, caught between a feather and a flower.
I'm shouting from the top of my voice,
from the foot of the stairs.
I'm talking to you from a squeak at the circus.
Pointing out opossum's breath.
Explaining, carefully, gunpowder.

I'm telling you the world is a fog of consciousness.
I'm telling you about the mountain chain
that's fallen in love with a river.
About a river pouring itself into your tea.
About a cup of tea embarrassed by the cosmos' antics.

You're listening to me spouting forth
from the swirling vortex in mommy's sewing machine.
You've been asleep under a stone for a thousand years.
You're hearing my voice, but believe it's the rain falling,
and that each cold drop is a planet or miniature Himalayas.

I'm talking to you from the ragged hum of my pulse.
I want you to realize that I'm snow

drifting in a far-off land.
I want you to see how the world still loves you.
To know the stars understand.

## Letter To Bill

A word sewn in the hem of the night.
A word sawing carbon phrases,
sowing a field at the end of the world.

Bill, it's four a.m. and I'm on the edge.
It's Sunday, with a fuzzy attitude.
March has gone out with the lambs
and is, I suspect, imbibing heavily.
The unseen looms in its dark subtraction.
Nightbirds are talking to the hand of God.
The stars have made their absence
into a statement, their intentions
the peculiar arithmetic of reason.

And, Bill, it's glum indoors,
this teeny metropolis wet to the bone,
weather our second skin, a cold draft
coming from the Ocean of Storms,
its little invectives slavering madly.

Erg by erg, we're moving
closer to pure existence,
heaven a breath in these rarified airs,
hell an idea to be let go of,
morning going up a hill...

And, Bill, it turns out
that wasn't a word I'd seen
but all our names rolled in a ball.
It was the ideogram for suffering.

## At The Appointed Hour

I was just talking to God.
He was sitting on his helmet.
He was pissing into the rosebushes.
Every other word was a world destroyed.
He mentioned he was fed up in Heaven
and longed to go it alone,
maybe start a business repairing furnaces,
invest in race horses,
breed showdogs on the side;
he said it was quite lucrative,
that the market was wide open.

No, you just missed him, a god's god,
about yay-high, steely-eyed,
icy fire where his hair ought to be.
We're playing cribbage next Friday.
We're going to a strip club,
and probably a few drinks after.

And he knows you, he said.
He's well aware of your little 'problem',
would really like to help you out,
but he's taken a pledge;
didn't elaborate much though.
And he's chubbier than you'd imagine.
*Too many cupcakes*, he confessed,
a bit sheepish about it too.

He was just in the neighbourhood
and thought he'd drop by.

At least that's what he told me.
And I can't imagine he'd lie about it,
not something petty like that.
I can't imagine he's even capable
of lying; or if he was
that he would or he did.

## Toyhouse

There's a horse in the church,
a frothing stallion, a mighty thoroughbred.
There's a mountain of isotopes. A used finger.
The little pieces that have fallen from you.

Inside our church is an inland waterway.
A many-storied candle. The cloak of the Egyptian.
The sexton never voices a care.
The lay minister is eating an onion,
the few shuddering cobwebs remaining
with the blood of the world on their hands.

We're a simple people, us,
our church a weed flowering on the side of a road.
Our church is a mop and a bucket.
It's the eternal wrangling with the infinite.
It's a toyhouse lined with leftover monkeyshine.
Like the right palm of Saturn.

Love reflects faith, which reflects religion,
our church a hall of mirrors, a strawberry blonde,
a perch for bladdered chaffinches.
This is when the dust settles in for a spell.
God has put his feet up and is reading a newspaper,
scanning the obituaries, chuckling unconditionally.

In this house it is we who are the visitors.
We're shaking the bonds of the human realm,
our church an ancient looking-glass.
It shows us who we are. Beleaguered moths.
Transitory angels. Lambs bleating.

# A Lifetime Ago

In a previous life I was Christ's inner light.
In a previous life I was a shoe heel in a window.
I was that red demon advising Nero.
A fold in a gown. A night at Versailles.
A triumphant horn-blat.

So many births, so many deaths . . .
But in a former lifetime I argued against time.
Time doing its odd little dance.
Time worming a hole in God's watch-pocket.
Time going headlong into the river,
pulling out the one I had loved,
pulling her out by the nails and hair,
placing her down gently at the riverside,
death's fish swimming in an ocean of air,
the mind devouring itself . . .

Recall any one of the previous lives
swept aside in the riptide of years,
details of which the soul does not willingly surrender.
Unresolved. Unremembered. Unshared.
More former lives than hot dinners.
Born again, again. Countless hosts of existences.
Legions of long-dead wives waving in the grass.
Waving goodbye to me, and the wars coming.
Waving come hither.

# Faraway Suns

*"And at night I love to listen to the stars. It is like
five hundred million little bells."*
*--Antoine de Saint Exupery, The Little Prince*

More stars than toads or moths or damselflies.
More stars than knots or wedding rings or roses.

From under my pillow I can hear the stars reflect
upon the 'hideous triumphs of function and form'.
They influence my moods and fads in furniture.
The tears of the stars are what water our vegetable gardens.

Black stars. Furnaces of indigo. Of indefinite colour.
Stars that creak in the wind. That create weather.
Fallen stars I collect like acorns or raspberries.
Aloof stars, haughty and remaining at a distance.
Copper stars on silver wires, suspended from the impossible.
Flowers of wordless fragrances gathered at the river's bend.
Little explosions taking forever to divulge their secrets
to the sleepy child, the fox, the worm and the hare.

A star-quelled night in a curious village.
I'm awake and listening to stories of epic proportions.
Tales of gods and animals, of eternal love and despair.
Saints wailing on a lush sward in Capricorn.
Souls in Aquarius singing an epoch-long mal aria.
Faraway suns, their arms burdened with purple planets.
Bright wells serving the will of the people, the strangest people,
who are very like us, and very much different,
who wish upon stars, studying their bones, and who wonder –
outlandish questions for which no answers exist.
Countless sums beyond number.

## Magnificent Whirlwind

When I think about squares I think about triangles.
Storm clouds trigger troubled thoughts on heavy metals.
Sunrise, to me, is a songbird singing down a mineshaft.

All my life I have been decidedly different.
All my life has been lived on an alternate Earth,
a glass planet, a world of soft green wood,

replete with sugar-animals, tin bugs and paper fishes,
with its moons on inside-out and back-to-front,
a world of garrulous continents and iodine seas.

Now I lie in an awkward position and put lights in the sky.
Every night is a god with a thumb in its mouth,
every dream a mathematical construction.

See? My laboured breath is a magnificent whirlwind.
I am pampered and made to suffer in turns.
Even the cat knows I am destined to live separate and alone,

that it's my curse to walk knee-deep in profound outrage,
my sole fate to marry hope unto horror.
That to exist is my wonderful burden.

# Heads In The Clouds

Astronomers, yawning at noon.
Astronomers peeking into a stone age dimple,
confusing roserock with frostweed.
Astronomers ringing the planets' chimes,
measuring celestial vibrations,
making a map from darker matters.
Bloody stargazers, they're up all night
jabbering over numbers in the kitchen,
climbing into a long cup of coffee,
made drunk with their own theories,
mad as a smashed lantern.

They have gone beyond vanity,
to the far shores of Iceni,
mystagogues getting it all wrong all right,
an entire cosmos of guessing-ness.

And because time is a ripped shower curtain
they think every moon is a football,
that every star is a whorish wink,
every nebula a suspicious rustle in an alley.
Because space is a bubble of time
the astronomers like to believe
they can behave like children.

I see they've lost their minds in wonder.
I see their poems are about everything
happening at once, each passing night
like a swift blow to the ribcage,
eternity an unanswered question.

Astronomers work in the darkest corners
of an ever-odder universe,
one foot on Meridians Planum,
and the other in the Pleiades.
Their wives take on a number of lovers,
their children abandoned to nature,
the otherworld tumbling over them.

But stacks of astrodynamics though.
Untold amounts of stellar capers to charter.
A great deal that's still unaccounted for.

Plenty of nothing.

## Space Between The Lies

Inane moon, madcap stars, cross-eyed planets,
Earth's gong thrumming in the salt and pepper lunacy,
the first night being also the last night,
existence circular in nature.

I'm on the light-path, one of the dark races.
I'm loving myself in a black mirror,
Deimos gesticulating, Phobos running not far behind,
Andromeda rattling her leg-irons,
gravity imposing its letter of the law,
atoms warring, space closing
like a door or an eye,
the ultimate silence thickening its broth.

My synapses sparkle and spar, mind delighted
with itself, its own divine machinations,
the universe a dull cliché, cosmos waterworn,
the Big Bang quaint in comparison –
like a cute little croft on Mare Frigoris,
say, or the red star of Christmas.

The space between the spaces expands,
while I gather in the far-off moments.
The infinite and eternal are wrestling quietly,
God in his heaven, or so I'm told,
a little brownstone bungalow
on the back steps of beyond.

All else, the miracle deepens.

## Is A Poem Fiction?

"Poetry is the only art people haven't yet learnt
to consume like soup."
—*W.H. Auden*

I'm writing about a forest of pins.
It's a poem underwater.
It's a book about sharp edges
and the wee wee hours.
A story about a story setting off
over an apparitional horizon.

Editor, please find enclosed
a borrowed vowel,
the infused souls
of dust-mouthed scribes,
the tale of the stone and the ballerina,
my dog-faced diary,
the chronicles of delightful bedlam,
the legends of squid . . .

I'm writing on a page
of frozen tundra, the moon
dreaming my verbs, mouse-thoughts
encircled within parenthesis;
like smoke rising
in a valley of icy alphabets.

I'm writing a thesis on silence.
A note reminding myself
about what not to forget.

Instructions on how to
take a rip out of the air.
I'm writing on a black envelope
with white letters.
(Suffering requires black lettering.)

I'm writing on my hand,
a parable gestating
at the back of my mind
for the past seventeen years.

There's blue blood in my pen,
and pencil shavings in my hair.
I'm writing without consonants,
Saturday unrolling its broadsheet.

I'm a book, I want to be read.
The real world a faint glow.
What's *actual* vaguely interesting.

I'm carving arbutus,
a calligraphy of fossilized sap.
I have an imageless imagination.

My God, I'm my own life sentence.

Dear oh dear, I'm the last of my line.

## Forgotten Promise

After the rainbow,
a pillow stuffed with dreams and mites.
A carnation dipped in gun oil.
A request from Death's neighbour.

After the rainbow, a meteor.
Scuffling among the cutlery.
A village swallowed by the countryside.
Spectres sparring.

The rainbow, painted on a cellar wall
by the blind sorcerer's daughter.
Under a tin bucket of milk.
Remote and indifferent
to men's strife and the causes of suffering.

After the storm, a rainbow.
Walking a tightrope. Twisting a wire.
Mocking the sounds we make
before nightly retiring.
As peculiar as lost money.
Like finding a finger in the snow.

The one that shows itself at night.
The deer's god and raven's deformity.
What the prisoner on the gallows saw
through the folds of his departure.

# Light's Wedding

# Introduction

*Mr. And Mrs. Invisible, shopping for celestial plywood.*
*Mother Inferior, stripping and strapping the naughtiest nun.*
*Captain Bulwark, tethering his airship to the sun's meadow.*
*Their adventures in many a magical realm.*
*Their investitures in the supernatural.*

*Aunt Gladiola's invincible marching band.*
*Cousin Thing-Bottom's wheel of delectable syndromes.*
*Uncle Uncle's expandable expendable mouse-soul.*
*Their long trek through the interior ghost-world*
*and how they overcame their unenviable lesions.*

*Mister Fudge's incorrigible antics throughout space and time.*
*Doctor Homebody's undeniably wild packages.*
*Professor Plot's set of his 'n' hers diurnal cavern-wraiths.*
*They being astounding in themselves;*
*having for some time conspired, but at great disadvantage.*

*Yes, these, and any other number of marvels dwelling herein,*
*replete with many astounding characters, places, things and events*
*proven here to be astonishing and of an extraordinary ilk;*
*including their numerous experiences, miracles and wonders.*

# Netherworld

This edge has no edge to it.
One of our echoes went out walking
and has never returned.
And what happens to the letters
and bright parcels sent there?

This bit is a ball bouncing.
This bit is a stick
running after a dog.
Which reminds me of cardboard
and zippers, of plantains
soaking in the dark brine of rum.
I'm thinking cocoa leaves and emeralds.

Because this hinge doesn't know
its moans from its groans.
It's like a meandering meteorite.
It's a blanket of moonstones.
It's a tool for smelling flowers.

You can see the confusion, can't you?
The once-gamesome now hagridden,
laid low by the choices of Man.
Like a planetoid's guts swelling.
The mass-illusions shattered.

And this part, which is the wrong part.
Its hidden chambers. Its lists.
Its secret door into the netherworld.
The wood badly warped from the sun.
And the drawers sticking.

## Ground Zero

In Nothingland, a cloud on the horizon
and stars burrowing under the void earth.
In Nothingland, a profound silence
the colour of air; and very low temperatures.

Nothingland, an imaginary supposition,
emphatic obscurity, a geographical trifle.
A place between two other places.
A slight theoretical conundrum.
A construction of paradoxical math.

Think of a holiday in outer space
or sweetened dreams of a sleepy dormouse.
Think of a million word long sentence,
but with nothing to tell you.

Nothingland, next door to Avalon.
Of dubious mass and dimension.
Of debatable purpose and girth,
its preposterous citizenry debating
the qualities of so-called reality,
asking so much of themselves
and receiving so little in return;
who need to refocus their attentions,
to find a point in the distance and just stare
at the whole of their insignificance;
inconsequential as it is, featureless,
and all around them.

# The Old Metropolis

The city was a ditch filled with brittle smoke.
The city was a nest of red-eyed spiders.
It had fur windows, blue fur windows.
It had leathery diphthongs,
like tassels, and a comet's brass railings.

I came at it from every direction:
glass runnels; straw drill-bits;
the swamp gas of its trillion mansions.

I went under it, using a pen to tunnel,
tripping over the grips and guy wires,
stumbling drunk in a broken-up wind,
swimming the noncompliant asphalt,
setting off early for  the nearest curb,
the city waiting, patient as a stone idol.

What is it about this particular town?
It's like the tides calling to our blood.
Gangsters here want to take you for a little ride.
Someone is always willing to pilfer your symbols –
by which I could mean any number of things.

But the city understands me.
While masked men and pickpockets feud.
While the moon rolls its cold silver.
While everything stops, becoming quite still,
and just listens . . .

## Fabrication

I'm building a cloud.
I'm fabricating ashen rain.
I have a velvety hammer.

This house will have a basement
at the top of a hill
This house will have snow walls
and watery windows.
And bone plumbing.
Tissues of wires.
Every room painted arterial red.

I'm tearing down whole forest fires
to construct a fold in time
and underground skyscraper.
I'm building a clot of sighs.
A city of attics.
All my cellars are bridges,
each willowy beam a hyphen
joining indiscernible words.

For nails I'll use nettles.
Fish scales for roof slates.
Sperm-based mortar.
Teardrops for tiles.

For all my years I have been
sawing into my life,
sawdust dovetailing sawdust.
All your time has been spent digging

a foundation in rice grains,
a cesspit we can't imagine.
All our lives we have been making
a fine coffin.

# The Puzzle-House

The wall is not a wall,
but wind off a lake.
The ceiling is a storm front
composed of shadows and din.
What you think of as a window
is a consensual hallucination
brought on by childbed fevers.

The house is two hundred years ago
and thousands of miles later.
For a front door, light playing
in the cold air of winter.
It knocks upon itself.
The key is in everyone's possession
and is made of water.
The Earth turns the key,
in the same way a mouth
eats its own words.
Only a pattering of footfall may enter,
and even these falter, uncertain.

But just who is it that lives here?
And where have they gone?

Imagine a honeycomb or labyrinth.
A house where the alcove and garret
exchange glances on the stairs.
The stairs, which only lead down
into the earthen bowels,
the soil itself the notion of a planet,

reality stacked like dirty dinnerware
in the flooding world-sink.

We stand in the hallway for eternity.
There's nowhere to go,
each room revolving on a separate axis.
The lightbulbs are brown suns.
The carpet a river of iniquities.
The mice gnawing the wires
not mice at all
but the fortunes of men.

# Open Invitation

Visit the ends of the earth.
Take in our ragged exhalations.
Stay inside the chalk circle.

Often I like to fly over the rooftops.
Often I am rowing
across a bay in a snowstorm.

I have salted bones
and mountainous breaths.
I have water on the mind,
every third wave a good idea.
I'm readjusting my storm surge.

Come, we can start a fire
by rubbing two worlds together,
by striking flint emotions,
by blowing on wind.
We can pitch our tent here,
its canvas octave, its silken penny,
its icy horseshoes.

Often I think I'm a river
and just wander around.
Often I am naked in the head,
sleeping from the neck down.

Why don't you forego formalities,
just drop in, have a good look around?
We can shop for shopping.

We can dine on compliments
while having our tickets stamped.

Often I fall by standing up.

Often I like to go down to the shoreline
and throw myself at the sea.

# True Nature

The empty house inside me.
The abandoned cars and cold churches.
Streets devoid of light and life.
Freed animals gone wild
in the undergrowth of an overgrown mind,
nature reclaiming itself, my true nature
taking the Earth back by force,
turning the world backwards
to a time before time, before darkness.

Silent rooms of the soul.
Dust mating with other dust.
Ash coupling with web.
Sadness sexing the sorrow.

Bu not even a shadow's shadow.
Not even the acidic sparkle of roach-breath
or bedazzled birds in the far-off branches.
Just silence colluding with quiet,
the sun scraping lichen from stone,
making a bone-powder, sand grinding
in the wind's gentle frenzy.

Where the ghosts are old,
older than God, than God's god.
The stars blinking out
and soil rising to meet them.
This old house in my head
tumbling down to the ground.

The human wars over.

The planet won.

## The Beautiful No

You begin drifting off,
soothed by sleep's sirens.
By the cradle
rocking in your mind.
A tuneless lullaby
pouring out of the woodwork.

Your eyes are weighed
down with building rubble.
A curtain is falling
in your world-weary dreams.
Your eyelids are guttering candles.

Someone once said
sleep is like climbing
under a barbwire fence.
That sleep is an island,
the undressed rehearsal
for a larger death.

Someone once went to bed
and never returned.

You continue nodding,
the executioner's basket
crying out for your head,
his pillow welcoming
the explorer home
from the farthest bournes
of light's bright empire.

Now, pigeons cooing.
Somewhere, dunes whispering
*Old sleepyhead.*
Everything's closing,
night's blizzard moving in,
the snowdrifts shifting,
the wind hissing up more wind,
its kisses numberless.

At the last hurdle
a dream stumbles,
its message unclear –
what is it saying
that only the heart can hear?

# Cries Of The Innocents

Trees going mad.
The ashram door inside me closing.
Fear shaving a plank.
Disenchantment at twelve o'clock.
Hate riding its pony backwards.
Dog-mind licking its tender genitals.
A fly alighting on your cereal.
Memories like bubblegum.
Your family skewered on an old bone.
Monsterisms in the bloodstream.
Daylight pouring out its invectives.
The cataclysmic bawling.

I think this is how the bee sees
or light meets a diamond's many facets.
I believe this is water merging
with other water, the two Niles
cutting into each other,
raindrops melding and forming a flood.

Or it's the many cries of the innocents
rising as one from the fire,
an unholy choir echoing in the rafters,
conflict mothering the invention
of prayer-wheels and the iron maiden.

I think this is death's handwritten letter.
It's causing an eye infection
and worm in the mind.
It's humming that same old song,
a tune infused with a viral decree.

And there's nothing nice about it.

## Last Night

Last night the fog tumbled out of the sea.
Last night was humbled by cottony textures.
The mist could be heard stitching tree branches
to sawgrass, sewing an unseasonable purple,
patching cloudbanks, knitting knots, weaving the air.
The wind could be said to be hopping pocket
to pocket, that it had quasi-angular piping
and the aftertaste of bottled hailstones.
That it sounded like coins dropping on the stairs.

Last night I was going dream-door to dream-door.
Last night I sensed a spicy aroma.
A fossilized plea swimming the channel.
A lunar raindrop. Mice in league with a hog's bristles.
Quantum packets of a miserable photon.

It was darker than midnight fifty feet beneath
the earth, the dead squinching their eyelids,
fear telling a story, camphor on its breath,
a wolf in its trousers, a kind of sleep burning.
In each nightmare they evicted me
from the house sin built under a hill.
Every breath came with an inevitable sad ending.

Friends, last night a tile in the floor lifted,
the damp getting into everything, sleet arriving
late, making a number of unreasonable demands,
combing the briarwood for youth gone missing,
winter solstice stranded on a higher plain,
the second coming inching closer,
spirits rearranging the tables and chairs,

building a stone house in my heart,
making the sound of water running;
water in exile and with nowhere to turn,
all the motions of the earth adjourning.

## Going Along

Plenty of nowhere. Driving instinctually,
the night red with moths' blood,
the road crossing and uncrossing its fingers,
the road like a icy gulch on the backside of Titan,
the half-moon crouched and growling
at an unseen stirrer in the woods;
which we pass through like a hot needle.

Life struggles under the briar rose,
wrestling with the clamps and hitches,
with the phantom snares set out for it.
I roll up the window, lest a shadow get in.
I turn up the crinkling radio,
the station tuned to the starfields,
night's vista in danger of cracking up,
of losing it altogether, the twinkling
nebulae and planets threatening to end it all,
and to take us down with them,
or wherever it is the cosmos goes
when the mind shuts, the eyes closing finally,
the light gorging on ultimate darkness.

I yawn, driving from instant to instant –
a singer missing the high notes in a silent opera,
a portal in my thoughts dilating,
unhinging my jaws to devour the Earth;
which is no bigger than a cherry now,
and sweeter than cream.

## True To Yourself

Darkness coming to cover the earth,
and I would rather be
a line from an old show tune,
flash-paper burning in a kitchen sink,
the unlikeliest parenthesis.

Soon night will be enveloping Beantown.
And I would rather farm dactyls
or manufacture oil-based jewelry.
I'd prefer to marry nation unto nation
or darn firemen's socks.
To be the world's left hand.

The sparrows return each evening,
flying from a hole in the ground;
and I pretend to be Saul's rain,
a cough in a cathedral,
a ringbearer wielding a rhinestone.
The stars are lamps primed;
so why can't I be a towering sunflower
or timed explosive?
Why can't I be a cat's paw in snow
or the burgermeister's walking stick?
The stars are pearls winkling,
and I want to be a deep voice
emanating from a soap bubble,
a wolf eating pie,
a glass of spiritual water,
a silvery shard of evidence,
the one dandelion in this world

that's found any solace.

In these last few hours
I demand to be allowed to be
dark matter scudding over Italy,
the paramecium's time machine,
an untranslatable passage,
a scar in the bark of a yum-yum tree.

I'm begging as fast as I can.
With all we know about to end,
why can't I just be *me*?
The one with the borrowed face.
The one with the camera for an eye.
The one with nothing better to do
and nowhere to go
and no name to speak of.

# Like As If

Is this the eye's needle or wind in a rag?
Is this a muslin hedgerow or a delinquent Roman numeral?
A cute little shillelagh, or is it kitty-kat porn?
Attila's airbrush or an ex-solstice window-shopping?
A damaged kidney or a spectre sleeping in a lawnchair?

I'm not quite sure if this is angel-wire or banana-bread.
I can't see if it's toothbrush-sweat or a rose's brow.
The tomato of solitude or a gnat holding in a breath.
A recipe for sheep or one twin murdering another.

Who can say? Who can really even see from here?
If this is the papal sandbox or a berry's crushed interior.
If this is a portable solar system or it's Scotland's chin-dimple.
A cola-flavoured bandicoot or the heart of the blizzard.

Or it may be just a wheel-clamp on its last legs.
A shepherd muttering oaths into his false beard.
A cantaloupe writing and re-writing a classical barb.
The chanteuse who comes in a variety of colours and forms.

Or it's only the wind talking, that would be more like it.
The wind struggling with the power and the glory of the word.
The wind talking the ear off a fluttering damselfly.
The wind telling a story and there's no one to hear.

Like a haywain at the top of a hill or tragic peanut butter.
Like a terminal sigh. Death's kiss. Fiery wishes.

# Us

We make sounds you can touch
and have seawater corkscrewing in our arteries.
We manufacture light
out of coat-tails and bobbins.
What you thought were the stars knocking
are bubbles in the brain's aquarium.
That isn't the fridge running,
we're turning wheels, it's the cosmos humming.

Million and million of hammers –
that would be the wind in the eavestroughs.
We resemble clothes strung on a line,
the ones that hang like hungry children,
that thump in the world's closet,
that ping whenever a bird flies near.
And they've placed a lightbulb
where our heart ought to be.

Too late, we're handing you the bill
for the peonies you believed to be pennies.
We're an intense memory,
not unlike a book being closed
or the Reverend's hankerings for seconds.
Very similar, if not identical,
to a phantasm spotted in the old glue factory
or an aftershock during a first French kiss.

When you call us, and you will,
the creatures of the forests stop in heed,
the Rockies shrugging, a homely girl looking

back before carrying on in the world.
We're more like whalesong
or a gas-jet waffling faintly.
We resemble mental blocks of wood.
We're quite wooly inside,
so when you hug us we're snug and cozy.
We've installed a platform in your life,
just because we can, because we wanted to,
it amuses us greatly.

Like sucking sparks from an exhaust tailpipe.
Like chewing stick-pins.
Like it's always been, if only moreso,
with all the attending whistles and bells,
the footsteps over your head
quite fanciful but leading nowhere

# Sing-Along

A song sung by the house dust.
A song to the spider's laborious thread.
A song in the tread of the emperor's carriage.

The mother weeping
over dishes in a kitchen melodrama –
she hears it, clearly.
The mercenary, cutting thick necks –
he hears it too.
The song of the blue chord.
The song of December transposed into June.
Of the wrong-headed angel.

Music plays on a stone adze.
It slips beneath the arctic waters.
It sits very quietly at the back of a classroom,
counting its glass beads and saints' knuckles.
Adjusting its badges and straps.
Accumulating dark knowledge.

You see the heart is an instrument.
The soul is a drum and a hand
pounding on the gates of a glassy heaven.
You see. The song is singing itself
in a night-stained doorway.
From out of the roof of your mouth.

A song about razors and cranberries.
A little song about a meteor shower,
about the rise and fall of dew.

The one we all sing, like wind under a rainbow
or chorus of doubt.

Beautiful shouting.

# Outcome

A rope bridge over a blank page.
The wind whistling Dixie.
Fallout gracing a walnut cabinet.
A clock doing the cha-cha-cha.
Benisons greasing their hair back.
Sailors frigging in the rigging.
A thumbnail sketch of a thumbnail.
A preacher converting a priest,
but the two of them consumed with envy,
sinners with time's blood on their hands,
the refectory broken free of its moorings.

You see, all the world is inside
this little red ball being thrown at a wall,
the entire Earth under a tea-cosy,
a whole universe, nuts and all,
flying through the hole in my shoe,
making a sharp left by the chestnut tree,
Polaris ad-libbing, Andromeda off-script,
the cosmos on a psychotropic bender,
waking in a smoky motel room,
lipstick on its collar, fingers aching,
a love-mummy under the oily duvet
making the sound two dollars create
when vigorously rubbed together,
a fifteen billion year old sinkhole
with lava-breath, comets in its hair,
a minor god clawing at moondust,
making a last grab at the ringpiece,
the aroma of rosinweed and rose moss,

stridulations of the katydid, tapeworms,
the whole nine yards and ball of wax
sucked down a drain, dragging light,
pulling the sky down, loosening firmaments,
taking desolation with it, devastation too,
holding even God under its ruined waters.

# Memorandum

You remind me of a ghost-town in flames.
Of a grey wolf in a playpen.
Of a bellows or riddles in cuneiform.

You remind me of the wounded flanks of Jupiter.
You're like someone who used to be famous.
Every time I see you I think about swans dying
and teardrops the size of Rhode Island.

You remind me of a snowball thrown at a hoedown.
You're very nearly the spit of the Khan.
Almost the exact image
of a rose petal dropped down a coal mine.

An emperor of small places,
I try to put you to the back of my mind.
I walk the dog of my heart
along the stormy breakwall.
I drink to get drunk in the spectral tavern.
But still you prowl the woods of my tongue,
still I'm reminded of harried mothers
up to their wrists in fetal blare.

It's uncanny, your resemblance
to a stinking, cloying, blinding smog.
Which reminds me of a childhood sweetheart.
That brings to mind a bear attack,
of which I can recall only random moments.

Honestly, you remind me of someone –

an old schoolmarm or a calendar girl.
My dead twin's uncle.
The sub-genius yelling at the crosswalk.

Or if not someone, then some *thing*.
An abandoned rocking-horse.
A rollercoaster crashed at the seaside.
A crater, unnamed, on the underside of Rigel Prime.
You're a lampshade, or a beach rumble.
A loose tooth in the maw of the wind.
A ceramic vase with its ribs caved in.
A manuscript stained with demons' come,
which is really stretching it, I know,
but I can't help myself, I keep thinking about you,
returning to the blue in your eyes,
how they remind me of a Saharan oasis,
the night smothered in stars,
little memoranda pinned to the darkness,
rumours of the ancients painting holes in the air.

Which reminds me, as well, of how much
you remind me of truculent airwaves,
of a bitch hound yodeling in a snowbound valley,
of a seventeenth century hiccup,
of moribund codfish and a reluctant heart –
the wind bowing down to the light of the moon,
looking deep within itself
and not liking what it finds there.

## Vague Sensation

What about the moon's bug?
Nettle-sting and stringy entrails?
The soul of the bulrush?

What about a whisper in a nunnery?
Copulating salt grains?
The painter's patch in a canvas chair?

We want to leave everything out
by putting it back in, by pulling it
down a clucking plughole.
We want to amass an army
of someone else's ideas and verbs.

So how about it, Mr. Mister?
A pun under a pillow. A pricked thumb.
The superannuated blood-letting.
Where each wound has two meanings.
Each word a summery ribbon,
a bowl of urine, a monstrous wine bottle.

O thought's vague sensations . . .
The tempest of glottal stops . . .
The outlandish simile's apparel . . .

What about a bustard inheriting a silver mine?
A mushroom attending the cinema?
Monotony's ring-finger?
An instrument for sleeping deeply?

How about 'all aboard' that slow black train

of garbled oaths and mangled metaphors?
And lean into those curves.

It is these, of all your riches,
you shall not surrender.

## Gifted

Given a vision in hands.
Offered a cruel notion.
Bestowed with ironic rubdowns.
Given the gift of sand
and a gaping void in the sternum,
making a fine thing from it too,
something now and new,
that leans toward the cockamamie
and which serves no purpose.

Donations of blood
are pouring in to our offices.
Red letters stuffed with bread.
Gog's head on a silver salver.
A hand-out of frozen fingers,
thread veins and bone wheedles.
The light's wedding presents.

Given a honeybee and derringer.
Given a ghost-laugh.
The gold-leaf rose.
Presented with Penelope's ice-pick.
A sniff of the Icarian Sea.
The char of carbon castanets.
A lachrymose insect.

On a planet most beneficent . . .
Conferred upon your heads
is sunlight brushing a candlewick,
a sigh granting you a brief reprieve,

and then it's back to your toil.
Or you're given a last chance
to strut over Heaven's abyss.
Thrown a spare bone.
Blown a few wet kisses.

Making of these things what you will.
Rushing into a problematical mind-set.
Attending to the higher miasma.
Building a fine house
in the good quicksand.

## The Morrow

The future is seven stories tall.
The future is wiping its eyeglasses.
A dark light at a hard window,
it's rifling through ma's spare coinage.
It flourishes in cold weather.
It has a newly formed mouth,
and from time to time attempts
speaking mock Esperanto.

This particular future *per se*
houses a disembodied super-ego.
The future Now will seem
like an old dinner or worn shoe,
its fortunes cyclical.
Cities there float on dream-matter.
Outer space is in its kitchen.
A last animal is to be crushed
by artificial sunlight.
Language vies, or it will, then,
with inter-personal religion.

Well, that's some theory, the future.
It's the fifth wall in a room.
A mountaintop epiphany.
Hypothetical wonderment.
Implosive nightmare.
You can, and you can't,
get here from there.

*Carpe diem,* miserable bastard,

the future is drawing nearer.
A censorious finger-sniffer,
its breaths are clouding your mirrors.
A cantankerous air,
it's screwing with the *axis mundi*.
Naked and ashamed,
the next future to come along
will be wholly self-aware.

That's when violence
tangles with starshine.
That's when Old Nick cuts off his beard
and the past begins over.

The same wars, but a new order.

# Terminal Moraine

Not unlike kissing a pig through a veil
or wolverine in a bridal gown.

Not unlike hearing
the plaintive cries of London Town
as the clocks turn back:
"Get your gingerbread here."
"Get your salop."

Not unlike the barefooted match-sellers,
the huskers of crockery-ware,
the street-sellers in the rain,
selling curds and whey in the heavy rain,
in the rain and selling flowers;
the women of silk, the women of rabbits . . .

Not unlike a burning prescience,
seeing the girl with the velveteen eyes,
the girl with the apes in her head.
Not unlike the astronomer
measuring Io's afterglow, then reduced
to a fistful of dirt thrown on a coffin-lid

When there were giants in the earth.
When there were gods deflowering youths,
and always the rain;
bringing to us life, bringing destruction,
each thunder crack a red crevasse,
each thunderbolt a demigod's
shortsword slicing a heel-tendon,

each fallen raindrop
an infant's grasp or angelic sigh.

Unlike now, its clockwise trappings.
The now before now, and the now after,
running late for the downtown train,
the gossip-mills in full production.

Where the eyeless feel their way around
by striking out violently and rockets glare red.
Where nausea rises, orbiting
like a planet's strangest satellite.
In forests of glass and light,
where things end on a fanatic's whim,
the long days of the immortals
merely urban legend,
our minds undoing their guide-strings,
the soul a bolus of rumours,
our hearts unbound
by the 'whirring fetters of imperfection'.

# Hung

Hanging from the moon is the Great Owl's neck-feather.
Hanging from the moon is a root's profile rendered in wax.
Because I said so. It behooves me. Because there it is,
a thigh muscle, grizzly sinew, a stretched ligament;
or I'm not exactly sure what it is, hanging from the moon:
an upside-down question mark with a thorn it its paw,
a renegade balloon-string, a shuddering fiddlehead.

Don't just take my word for it, son of a bitch,
go and see for yourself the gossamer webs,
like rays of milk or bent car-radio antennae,
like shaved heads of the condemned, like saucy garments.

You can almost believe it –
that hanging from the moon is the twenty-seventh letter.
That hanging from the moon is a disembodied housecoat,
a sliver of drool, pink pants, an unpaid gambling debt.

Hold your horses – it's actually a runaway moonbeam.
It's a ladder of frozen exhalations.
The pathway to enlightenment,
but very few are willing to accept it,
the Nothingness, but with dimension and breath.
Like a soldier's ribbons. Like ancient death.

# Conscience, with Fur

# A River Running Underground

In my mind is a paper mountain.
God shrugged, and that was my mind
separating one water from another water.
My mind imagined other minds.
It manufactured an idle daydream.
It made shadows after dark,
creatures without substance and form,
glass cities, ethereal fogginess,
the most beautiful of all the monsters.

In my mind is a sun weeping light.
Sparks star off an iron spike
while my mind paints jungle flowers,
highways of ice, celestial filaments,
an army of children crying:
"Toys and snowfall at Christmas!"

A vortex of quiescence,
and my mind is resting by a calm lake.
A storm's fury and human furor
and my mind is wandering in a thick forest.
The universe is a single great thought,
my mind asleep on its downy pillow.

Where nothing, and no one, may wake it.

# The Mind's Blue

Have your mind create a stone-shaped rain.
Celebrations of bruised velour.
A pelt of goblins' wort. Spires and classrooms.

Have your mind think about Ptolemy's giggle.
A chapter of anvils in a meteor swarm.
About infinite rounds of canasta.

Think of flaming ant-breaths.
Of a scowl in a runaway carriage.
Invent green panthers. Carboniferous sighs.
Shakespearean flannel.

Get your mind to configure a long walk in the sky.
Make it do diamondy cartwheels.
Think of love's gossamer muscle.
Attempt to see with only the mind's blue eyes.

It's like a headache, this thoughtfulness.
It's like a space that craves filling.

So think your tender centipede-ideas.
Have the mind sketch the mouth's inscription.
Place a cosmos at the front of your head:
where the gold rings of the sun's works
turn and every notion and whim are stirring.

Go on. Ponder quantum loopholes.
Mull over that bloody death wish
you've been meaning to have.

On finger-cymbals tickling a rift.
About what the lions imparted to Daniel.

Think like a soupbone and burning mission.
Think like a fox-cry or pinking shears.

Like a phosphorous bridge.

Or love ascending.

# Just Think About It

In this book, blood in the rain,
and you can't buy decent shoelaces.
In this book, the three graces,
Beauty, Delight and Chastity,
sharing a profane liqueur.
And shamans in the wallpaper,
real honest-to-god miracle-men
and women of extraordinary comeliness.

In this book, a city of gold letters,
of black velvet letters, letters
of fire, leaking like a gas mains,
sinking like slabs of concrete in the harbour,
spun like windmills of knife blades,
singing like a dog in a cornfield.

This book, filling the pages up,
pouring oil into the Word.
Which contains nuts and lemons.
That holds a permit for a pistol.
Ghostwritten in the third person,
you can read it in the dark,
its fancywork, its arty sorcery.
You can finger its sentiments,
tears catching in your throat like fish hooks.

This book values a clear complexion.
It's lost in a forest at night,
caterwauling in the flowerbeds,
sewing grass seed, stirring a pail

of poems minus punctuation,
of lunar etchings, fiscal reportage,
leftovers of burnt offerings,
remnants of the mouse's tale.

This book lives in a faraway village
where stainless steel snowflakes are falling.
A fanfare greets its each sneeze.
It has a horse's head and fish's body.
It doesn't know what it means
but it's really chewing it over,
a thing as desolate as it is divine.
Think of a taxi waiting at the curb
or pyrex vial of dodgy insulin.
Think of a yes saying no
or ship sinking in a bottle.
Think of a book thinking.

# Between The Temples

I'm thinking of a number
between four and five.

I'm thinking of a green moon
and fluffy-galaxy pastry.

Of a dalliance with glass
beads and go-carts in flames.
Of the church's goose-egg
Its moody palomino.

I'm thinking of homespun indigo.
Of the bright pain in the world's eyes.

I'm just cogitating, you know,
and the consequences be damned.
Musing and sulking
in my underground lair,
in my concrete pillbox,
among stars printed on a kerchief.

I'm thinking very hard
about thinking very hard.
About the futuristic millions.
About silver talents
and magnesium god-hammers.
Of how much I need you
to think of me not thinking
about you and what you're thinking.

My head hurts from being
banged against the sky.
That's my brain that's imploding,
its funky bubble, its jumbled imagoes.

Can't you feel its purpled fuzziness,
so soft and so shiny?
Can't you hear its spurs clanking?
Its cascading hoof beats.
The wind under the staircase.

Can't you hear the word in your ear?
And the mind snowing?

# Art, For Pete's Sake

Mondrian's tree. *What about it?*
I was just looking at it. *And?*
I was just thinking. *Yes, you were.*
It's very . . . treelike. *It's very like a tree.*
But it isn't a tree. *No, it isn't.*
As if from life, but once removed.
*Art is life at a remove.*
It's not the real article at all, is it?
*It's not really real, no.*
The hand copies what the eye sees.
*The hand, I'd say, copies the mind.*
Of course! Which copies what the eyes see.
*Pretty much. Tree. Eye. Mind. Hand.*
And the actual painting itself.
*And there's that too.*
The five stages of art.
*Or the five levels, plus the viewer.*
And their eyes, and their minds.
*It's getting complicated, isn't it?*
Surely. Then it must be difficult to be
"genuine" as far as the artist is concerned.
*Perhaps "impossible" is the word;*
*the original subject-tree could be*
*thought of as genuine though.*
And here I thought it was a painting of a tree!
*Or very like one.*

## Some Dreams Are Sweeter Than Others

In one dream I had
a white dog followed me
through the porticoes of Hell.

Ah, the slight sensation of things . . .
The unholy terror.

And yet in other dreams,
a bible on fire,
rips in a rainbow,
a star down a well.

One star, from the sift of heaven,
and the countless others . . .

In a dream I have still yet to dream,
are seraphim joyriding, their jaws clenched,
their buttocks, their fingers, too;
the ballast of sleep
priming night's cold furnace.

And then the World Dream,
consisting of two dreams
and which I cannot fully embrace.
So that I awake three times,
my eyes opening like a mouth,
my eyes clear and looking
around the corners of *mind*
for something that not ought to be found,
my dream become a night-bird
and it lost to the gathering darkness
and sea's ravenous swell.

## Misery's Supper

Empty out your burdens
Make a new mind.
Wield hope like a weapon.

You're the dark in a cavern,
the restless winds tearing
through a chink in time,
time married to other time.
A thought crushes your temple.
A tremor beckons.

Then arise, sir mouse,
and enter the dun cathedral,
the coliseums of flare.
Arrive swinging like mad,
like wow, like whatever,
Cast off the sky-metaphors,
your hatful of bandages,
your galoshes of kohl.
Say 'of', little friend.

You're a line on a road.
A word on a billboard.
A spike through the head.
You're love's riot.
An incendiary keyhole.
The lingering dust in a shed.
Drink deeply
from sorrow's cupped hands.
Dine on misery's supper
then sleep like the dead.
Or even simpler, walk away.

Become as a salt stronghold
in the mind's Sahara.
Construct an oversoul
from ashes and glandular stench.
Run down the corridor
your dreams have painted red –
so long ago now
the archangel named Death
can scarcely remember.
Become as if unsighted,
a rumour feeling for an ear,
your teardrops pressed
of their briny wine.
Become as if one sleeping.
Untroubled. Unstirred.
Always on the cusp of awaking.

## On The Wall

In the mirror is a mudshark and tithes of amnesia.
In the mirror, a face with nine fingers.

Every crack in the mirror is a quiet millstream,
the fishes outnumbering our names for the damned.

Posing, I notice a life lived backwards.
I can hear the Sirens tempting me nearer.

Looking, I find I've the pale face of Luna.
I see its infamous hare bounding.

The sea in the mirror is quicksilver and lime.
It's an interstellar harvest, distant and cold.

The mirror's reflection offers little asylum.
There's no refuge for children or the insensitive.

The mirror is a dove's feather or whale's spout.
It's a Venusian volcano, a glass of dandelion wine,

a planet sown with methane thunderheads.
The mirror is a rip in Zeus's fabric, a wishing-well,

where each coin becomes the mirror itself,
where each request serves as its own reply.

Reach in and lose a hand. Walk into its fogbank
and you'll not return. You won't remember.

# The Blank Leading The Blank

Two versions at loggerheads in a fuggy bar.
Bloodroot and bloodstone mistaken for one another.
A mirror preening in another mirror.

All day I have been going in and out of a door.
I've met myself coming around a corner.
I've taken to using another man's name,
putting on his shoes, his face, his wardrobe.
I keep waking up in two worlds at once.
I've entered the era of twinned sewers fuming.

Help me out of this farrago of entangled incidents.
Give me a third hand and irony's deep pockets.
Assist me in my wonder.

Because all day I lay beside myself.
All night long I have been getting in and out of a bed.
I'm in a dream, but can't get my eyes to shut.
Now I'm a pair of meteors bumping noggins.
Now I'm a couple of slightly befuddled breezes
meeting in the English countryside.
I'm actually my own shadow.

Honestly, I was just trying to shake my left foot.
I was thinking about death sleeping,
of that which turns by not turning.
Before the lie came to earth and white married red.

Outside, the snow is calling a stranger's number.
The dark and I are writing on his window,
an infinite fashion of loops and curlicues,
a collective *we* administering to the self's torture.
Our smokes merging.

# A Man Of Substance

All his days are spent
among the apple-headed legions,
the fault-finders, the oblique,
the money-lenders;
among the heartless rosebeds
and monasterial chanting;
amongst dogwood and briar.
He assigns the clouds
new and more difficult patterns.
Light rays dance in his matted hair.

You're in a city made of water,
and this is his mind,
what his mind represents
at any given moment.
As crazy as a shitepoke, they say of him.
As mean as cats' meat.
As pale as a fish.
Or you'll find he's arguing the horns
off the devil, bartering over a truism;
as did his father's father before him.
Living a life like a hearse
burning in a field of rape
or puff of expensive cigar smoke.
Like the eighth seal being broken.

See? He's got a face like spilt soup,
a very grim and hang-dogged expression
he'll often hurl at the feet of the sea.
That static in your earpiece is him chewing.

I am sorry, but you both share the same name.
The two of you call to one another,

and yet you both seem surprised.
You pretend to having been born sightless.
He's playing the harmonica sadly.

# Green Sun

You continue along the left-handed path.
You enter Troy smoking.
Or perhaps it's a pre-Cambrian scullery.

Your body demands minute morsels of pecan pie.
Your heart is the moon waning.
The mouth, as per usual, is talking trash,
sprinkling a fine dusting of minutia,
junk attracting junk, the mind's dragoons
attending to other, more soporiferous, matters.

So that's where you are, in Mars' basement.
On a field of blackened dew.
In the France before this France started.

I see you going up and down light's ladder,
milking sentiment, shunning playfull repartee,
skimming Beelzebub's burgeoning billfold;
the gendarmes and free press all wise to your scam.
I hear you knocking on the present tense.
You're at the Earth's back door.
You're challenging a grunion –
although Lord knows why or what it means.

We share the same headache,
the exact thumbprint, the one bed.
It's like I've been kidding myself for centuries.
It's like you're me,
if but for only every other heartbeat.
We have identical ideas
burning down in our head.

We both end badly.

# Go-Betweens

Ravishing the dream-vault.
Burning down Thought's cellar.
Light nailed to the mind-attic.
Ram-raiding consciousness,
a bit of psychic window-shopping,
taking down the last minutes,
examining closely the god-scat
for any blood or sign or mystic seed,
scanning laborious passion
for a single golden kernel
among all men's follies.

But then ghosts enter
through a crack in the house.
They come carrying sacks of spuds,
with wheels and wheat
in their lattice of hands.
Ghosts storm under the floorboards,
taking small bites out of what it was
that I was thinking,
putting names in their boney mouths,
deriding my efforts,
arguing with the house-dust,
go-betweens for suffering and sorrow,
bent on darkness, its purest definition,
how precisely it applies
to the conscience, to art and the will.

Ghosts speaking in tongues
to the blue-assed flies.

Ghosts mocking love's letters,
setting out before me a daunting task,
hunting this end-line for anything
resembling common sense
or a wrong decision.

## Of A Ghostly Appearance

You're one of those apparitions
flitting in and out of the mind's house.
An apparition with an upside-down scream,
that has an emptiness where its soul used to be.

You're that apparition haunting the loess dunes,
hooked on a monastic wind,
blind-black terror caught in your craw.

One of those apparitions made up
of thousands of smaller apparitions,
with a voice like a golem digging a trench,
a laugh like a sliver being torn out,
breaths stinking of an icy cistern.

Didn't I see you phosphorescing in an alleyway,
your heart being carried in a ghost-dog's jaws?
Wasn't your father an hallucination
and your mother a shimmering heat-mirage?
I'm sure I heard you dragging a foot along.
I'm sure I heard a granite monolith
being bullied aside.

Oh, you're not an apparition,
you're merely dimensionally impaired,
your weeps like rain in the grass,
your cries like teeth grinding.

But what a face! As if water pouring down a hill.
Like a slapped ass. Like the moon fallen over,

# Some Angelology

Angels sifting blood from blood,
exposing their beatific underthings,
aswim in light's I-beams.
Angels writing Death a mash letter,
romping among day-glo altocumulus,
breaking weather, baking sorrow's bread.

Angels of swamp and ghetto,
hovering beside a foggy car crash,
possessing a flower's temperament and temper.
The angels of indigestion and football.
The angels of stones dropped
in the ocean or flung at the sky.
The angels moonlighting as messengers.
Mobs of angels rioting, rebelling,
flashing ethereal handguns,
in sharp skirts of leather and chrome,
the Almighty's will the last thing in mind;
angel-mind part foam, part thorn,
rank humans their emotional betters.

Because angels argue with time
they have inexhaustible dudgeons.
Angels are filling up the hollows
with the rainwaters of form and energy.
Pulling on the starlings' advances,
drugging our well water, dervishing always.
They consume their weight in thunder,
blushing like a blackened rose,
half-drunk, smoke issuing from their loins,

gliding to the far end of Forever,
riding the celestial zephyrs
that blow this way and that way
on the back of the moon.

You're sitting on their communal lap.
They run their fingers under your sweater,
tugging on their heavenly bits,
knotted to God's infinite locks –
oh, the mention of God,
which has them twisting their haloes,
burning as martyrs burn, pawning feathers,
hurling devilish invectives,
throwing the bricks and bottles of tantrums,
huffing and stamping their feet;
their small and perfect footsteps
making the sound of snow when it falls.

# A Snowball's Chance

It's snowing houses and darkened offices.
It's snowing torn paper hearts,
a blizzard of bluebells and teats.
There's snow up to my third eye.
It's drifting on Mare Librium.

I'm trudging through night's white-out.
There's minus zero on my breath.
In my mind is a coat of thick black fur
and mammothy mittens.

It's cold. It's dark.
And yet from everywhere comes light.
Sky, sea and earth are all of the same.
It's you who dares draw back a veil.
It's you who's warming their hands
by the hearth's dulled flames.

You see a stranger come to visit,
a dark-hearted snowman
pulling clumps out of the world's hair.
We grew up together, remember?
We set fire to the schoolhouse,
we were that frozen.
We used to joke about snowballs
and dine freely on icicles.
We swore it was June in January,
moving Valentine's Day to the ninth of July.
We promised ourselves a snow mountain
and fountains of time.

And yet, only horizontal wind-chill.
An arctic bash of suburban ice ages.
The rictus of a hard winter.

# From A Frozen Planet

I remember a wedding on Fornax.
The juices of Cepheus.
A girlish sneeze in the Virgo cluster.

I remember every third star was bent
on getting home before dawn.
The smudged thumb of the universe.
A calm in the eye of the mind's storm.

It was warm for midnight,
the gods' dog, Sirius, snarling,
asteroids taking their star turns,
dark matter spangling the ozone.

Light kicked holes in night's imperfections
and the candy-canes of Sagittarius.
Red-headed Mars was over the moon,
Neptune cradled in a willow's arms,
being gently soothed, rocking back
and forth to the music of Time.

I remember a cosmic spider and galactic web.
The carbon rills in Perseus.
Mispronouncing, twice, Iapetus.

I recall a night so quiet
you could hear the planets thinking
and a sulphur-slide on a faraway world.
I remember a last gamma-ray
before daylight barged in,

before morning's boast and courage,
before the sun's brash glory
overshadowed everything, the something
which was nothing, but wasn't.

## Tao And Zen

She was sitting at the foot of the world,
talking to the sun in her head,
meditating upon a soul-flower.
She was tracing a vein to the source of its blood,
lowing in a manner fashionable to cows –
no, she was confusing cows with crows,
battles with beetles, sunlight with sin.

Soon a calmness descended,
a glowing cloud of unknowingness.
Inside her mind was a rogue moon
looking for a place to throw down its blanket.
Smoke issued from her pores and ears.
One of her dimples whimpered.

Outside, the Age of Anxiety roared.
But inside, toasty and warm,
the girl dragged a single toe
through the marshes of her bubblebath.
She inhaled Tao and exhaled Zen.
Tarry constrictions in the capillaries
began their slow deconstruction.
Kosmos shifted an inch.
Demons turned tail.
The war with moonlight ended.

The girl sank deeper in perfumed loam,
up to her thighs and other limits.
Visions perpetuated themselves.
Love came bursting through the cat-flap.
Everything, or so faith promised us,
was going to be just fine.

# Drunk On Love's Bathwater

*"Thy lips are like a thread of scarlet."*

My love is a hand of flowering aces.
She wears an overcoat made of tumbling tides
and the expressions of demon-genius.

My love is a cowboy ballad.
She was slit by God's knife.
A blood-trail leads from the garden's gate
to a hole in a floor in a brothel,
where she has made a house in the dirt,
her former school a hair shorn,
her stifled laughter vermilion.

My love is a fissure in the earth.
She's like a tremor beneath the sea.
Her Easter bonnet is filled with rainwater.
She wears powdery panties.
In her heart is a cross burning.
Her glance is a perpetual bedroom.

I met her in a car accident.
In a Scythian bun-fight.
Behind a closet of fine linen.
We took turns taking turns;
first the crow, and then the scarecrow.
There was glamour all over her breath.
We thrashed about in love's muck.
Our ardour harried the earthworm.

Then lust wasted its candle,

my love cavorting with Oden and the milkman.
She was the mother of twin psyches.
This road we're on is her soul.
Were I to lose her in a crash
I'm sure the sky would fall from itself.
If she were to succumb to divine intervention
what could I do or want to undo?

Perforce I'd run her through
or set sail with my ghastly armada.

While for ten years Troy was held under siege
and the unborn were heard to be weeping.

# Affair Of The Heart

Loving you is a dangerous word.
It's like having plasma orgasms
or a fish in the bowels.
Loving you is a purblind bus driver
joyriding in the Peruvian Andes.
It's a sack full of sorry.

"Me loving you is not the same
as you loving me,"
said the hawk to the manatee.
It's more like a wedding cake
in a wheatfield. It's like chatter.

Love is one car crash
crashing into another car crash
or a charge of army ants
swarming a dead donkey.
A cartoon caper, my heart
goes up with a rocket
and comes down with a *thud*.
A comic forgetting his lines,
my heart is an eagle
catching horseflies.
A fist through a mirror.
A lost ticket for the lottery.
One of us is going to have to stop
lying to themselves.
One of us is going to
have to flee this
crumbling coliseum

that once was our love.

We can't even tell ourselves
apart in the dark.

Which one of us is the lovelorn god?

Which of us is the burnt offering?

# Charging Into The Vacuum

Tomorrow, Mr. Voice, everything will be different.
*Oh, and how do you mean; and please pass me the pineapple.*
Well, first of all, it will, perforce, be very unlike today.
Dawn's introduction will be accompanied with a kettle drum roll.
The shadows will lengthen; if only indiscriminately so.
*Yes, the shadows, they're prone to change; much like the weather.*
Exactly, Mr. Voice, little changes become a revolution.
*And change alone is unchanging; would you have a napkin?*
Of course, how thoughtless of me; but tomorrow this'll all be gone,
the moment, the light, emotions, deeds; it all shall pass.
*And a spoon, dear friend, a spoon would be quite handy.*
Once again, Mr. Voice, I have been remiss; you will forgive me,
I've been preoccupied lately, unhealthily so,
my attempts at creating balance only inventing more imbalance.
If my life were a ship at sea I fear I'd be sinking . . .
*It's only natural to equip one's self for a world that no longer exists.*
Precisely, that's just what I was explaining to my barber.
Why, it was only the other day we heard our shared future come a-knocking.
*We're all dreamers, it seems, Mr. Voice; we're all dreaming the dream.*
*And now to work. And now to remember our dreams.*

# Tiny Apocalypse

The One is marred by circumstance.
Prostrate to a higher power,
the One is making it rain,
a cinema of tear-fall and bad water.
Let's throw it a crust or a rind,
teasing it mercilessly.
Get the One to cry, a draconian sobbing,
every seventh tear a pearl or lava-bomb
on the fiery slopes of contention.

The One attends to moth-eaten despair
and is sipping from eternity,
from pools of lavender,
a tiny apocalypse
emanating from its slackened mouth.

The One, divvying infinity
into smaller and smaller quantum packets,
building sweet 'n' sour mysteries.
The One making a frantic dash
into the utterly fantastic.

A minister of rag and bones.
The kissing-stick tyrant.
An auditor of bricks and tin.
The One with the skewed perspective
and momentary lapse of reason.
The One knocking
on your forehead's door.

It has a soot-marred underbelly
and wine-stain for testicles.
For a voice, a string of planets.
Its breasts are pendulums
perfectly keeping four/four time –
it's us who are out of step,
it's we who are debasing the centuries.

We're the problem.

# The Art of Listening

I hear two moments conspiring.
A needle hanging by a thread.
A voice in the cornfield.

It's three a.m., four a.m., five.
I hear the angels' triumphant reveille.
Airplanes crashing into the sky.
Moldering reels of audio.
My inner dog is barking.

I hear the song of the mute and night's lyrics.
The alfalfa speaking to the swinging scythe.
Morningsong's brilliant hammering.

Listen up. Listen closely. Listen hard.
Satanic code and ricochets.
A sign creaking in a windstorm.
Shoe-squeak. Miniscule wedding bells.
A spectral alarm. The tiniest drum roll.

I hear the pronoun curse the adjective.
The adverb argue with prepositions.
A noun shouting its proverbial proverbs.

I can hear, if I can't see,
the immediate speech of stuttering interpreters,
an owl's hoot and coyote howling,
lisping falsetto and jabbering twang;
that which we needed to hear
but most dreaded hearing.

I can hear the salt on your tongue,
the ash of your kisses.
I can hear the little red pump
of my heart's geography.
A sprinkling of profanity.
A bride squealing.

I'm *listening*, but I'm not listening.
To glockenspiels in a leaden downpour.
Comic shenanigans. Sneezes stifled.
The drunken spoon-maker rattling his wares.
I can hear the discordant and minor chord
of a poem ending, here, at the end
of sleep's long corridor, on the heels
of so many words.

# Huge Quiet

The quiet, an abrupt stillness
resting in a sun-driven glade,
parlaying a few cursory gestures
to the bats inside my head
before putting on its paper slippers.

The quiet, without much purpose,
hobbled by self-restraint.
Visiting Earth in the guise of a draft.
Challenging the vacancies.

Am I expected to judge
the little spaces between noises?
Shall I conclude that it's silent
because of what I don't want to hear?

Which is? The quiet,
in the crib of a woolen judder,
verbs and birds in its unkempt hair.
The mouth's wound healing nicely.

A sound like sea fog or bamboo leaves
or two tinctures exchanging presence.
Like sleep singing to the mole
or doll laid out beside a phony pretense –
deaf long before the Enlightenment,
mute since Crusaders cut out its tongue,
halt for untold centuries . . .

The quiet, the salt of her vinegary kisses,

her lips cracked and pried apart.
And wise too, granddaughter to the oracle,
wisdom running deep in her veins,
her bloodless and straw veins.

What it wants from you can never be written.
What it's asking of you can never be said.

# About The Author

The author apologizes, but is unable to reply to correspondence personally.
The author is a human shipwreck spilling his guts out onto the beach sand.
The author is sometimes a licked stamp, and sometimes an X on a broken treaty.
He's an insult scrawled along a lemony yellow outhouse wall.
He gets a penny a page. His signature is slanted. His books are burning violently.

No one takes the author seriously, the boy with the sun in his eyes,
that guy with the hole in his heart, the last drunk standing. You know,
that fellow over there that's on fire. Last seen hanging from a streetlamp
and his readership outraged. Last heard calling from a phone booth
at the corners of Wattle and Dung. Once mentioned in passing.

The author would like to take this opportunity to thank the editor
for kindly whisking his family away to relative safety.
The author has been translated into Senegalese and Pawnee.
You might have read his roadkill cookbook. His revisionist Bible of Hell.
His novels pulped to mulch. His poems lining an old shoe.
The scraps of faintly lined paper, made into little paper bells from a reader
lost in Iowa. Or maybe it was Kansas.
Read each poem as if it were a valentine to death itself.
They're like funny snow falling. Like the Devil's dandruff.
Or leaves from a tree squawking.

*Some of these poems were published previously in the following magazines : Arsenic Lobster; Ascent Aspiration; Caught In The Net; Dark Matter; Diverse Voices; Dossier Journal; Eskimo Pie; Exercise Bowler; ExFic; Fat City Review; Gutter Eloquence; Hamilton Stone Review; Harbinger Asylum; Heyday; The Inflectionist; The Journal (UK); Mad Hatter Review; Melancholy Hyperbole; Mel Brake Poetry; Metazen; North American Review; Oxford Magazine; Paradise Review; Petrichor Machine; Poetry Kit; Poetry East; Poesy; Point Blank; The Potomac; Pure Francis; Rattle; Red Booth Review; Regime Magazine; SubTropics; Theodate; Vein; Verdad; The Whistling Fire*

Pski's Porch Publishing was formed July 2012, to make books for people who like people who like books. We hope we have some small successes.
**www.pskisporch.com.**

323 East Avenue
Lockport, NY 14094
www.pskisporch.com

Proof

Made in the USA
Charleston, SC
14 September 2016